T5-BSG-832

STECK-VAUGHN
NEW WAY
HEADS and TAILS

Meet Meg

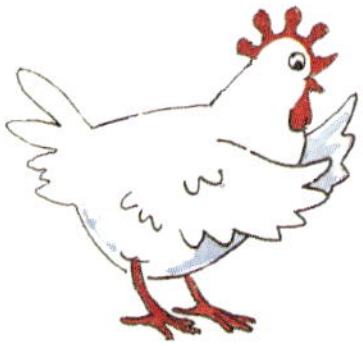

STECK-VAUGHN COMPANY
A Division of Harcourt Brace & Company

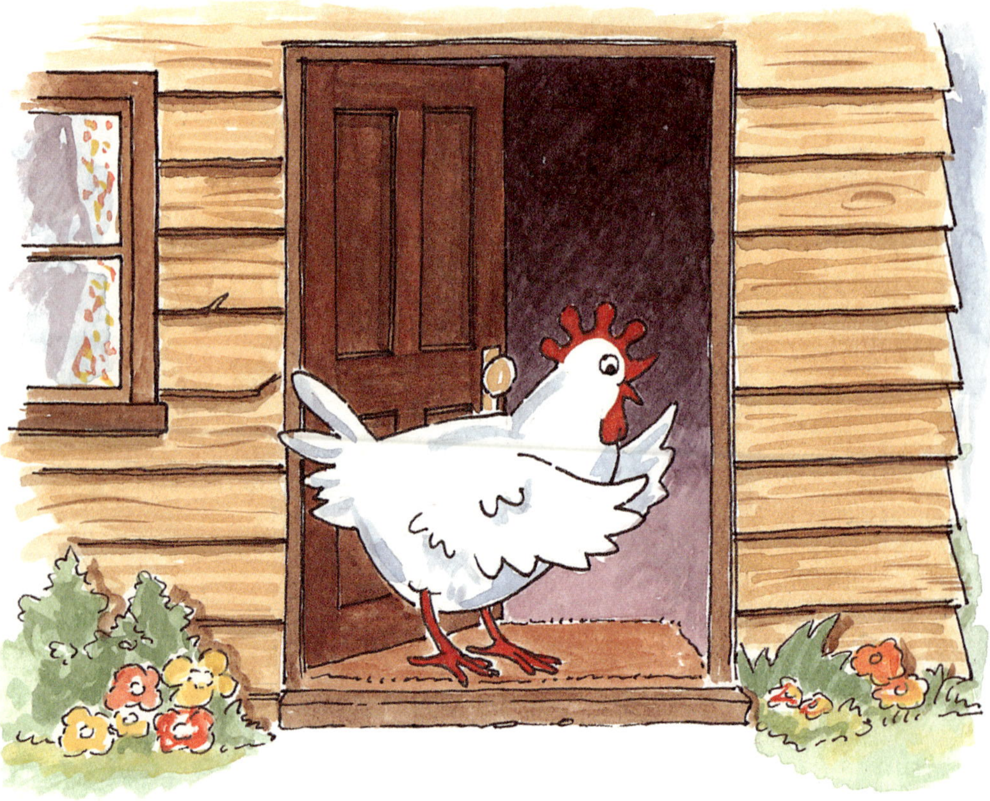

This is my home.

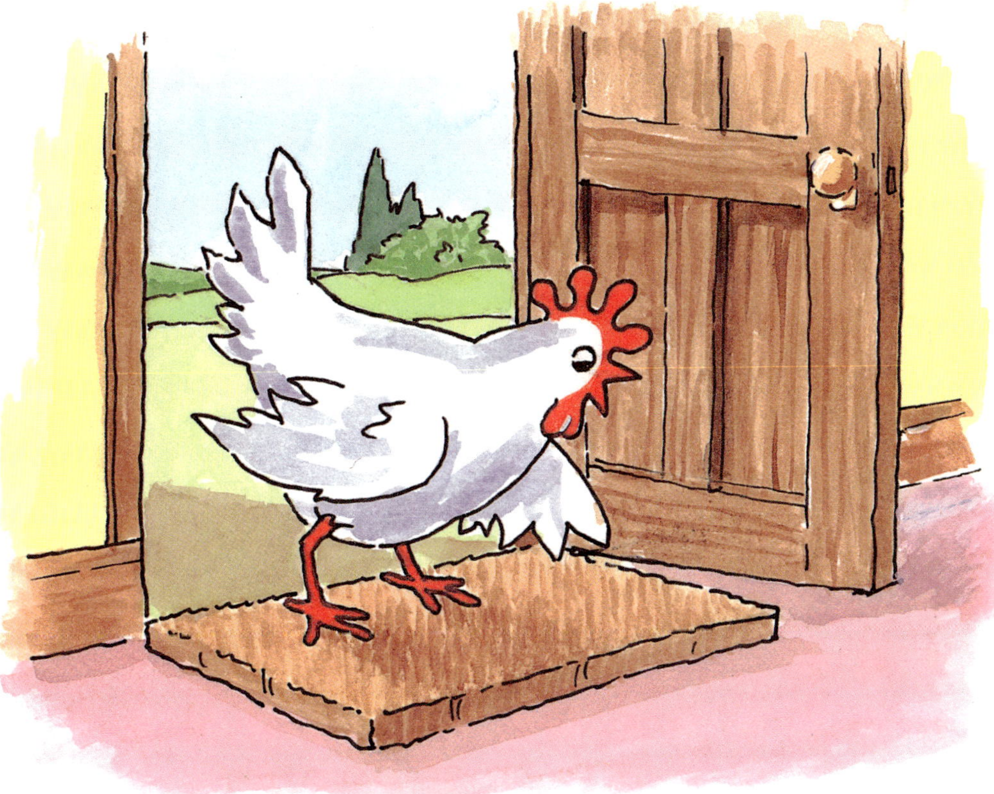

This is my mat.

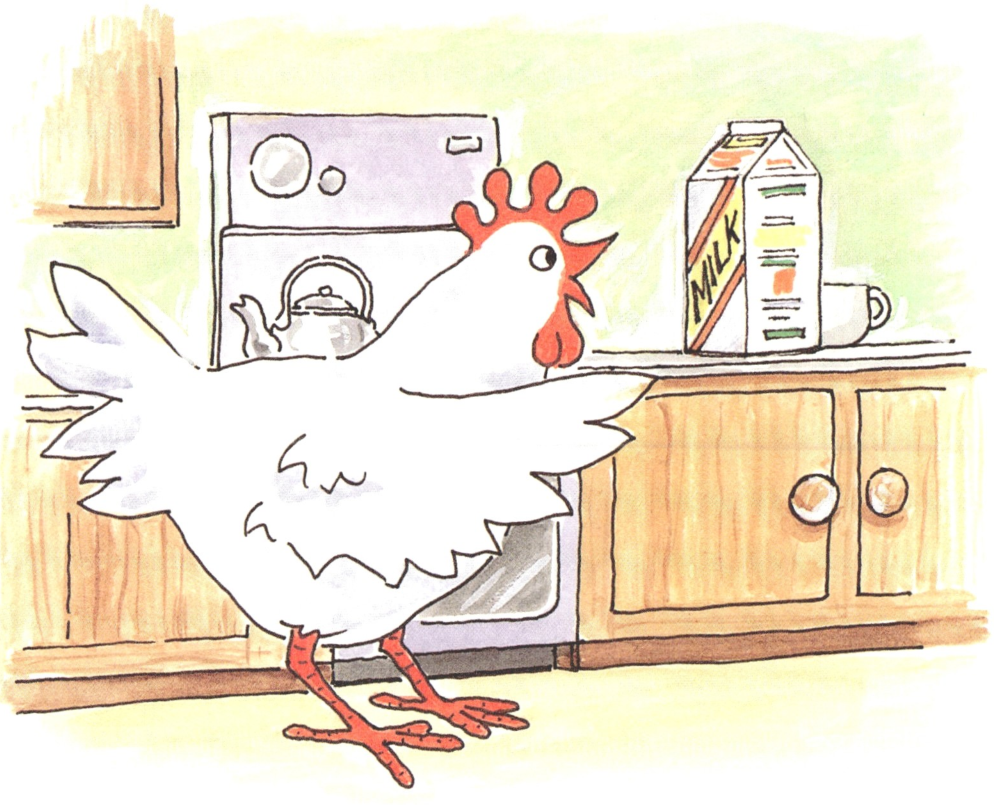

This is my milk.

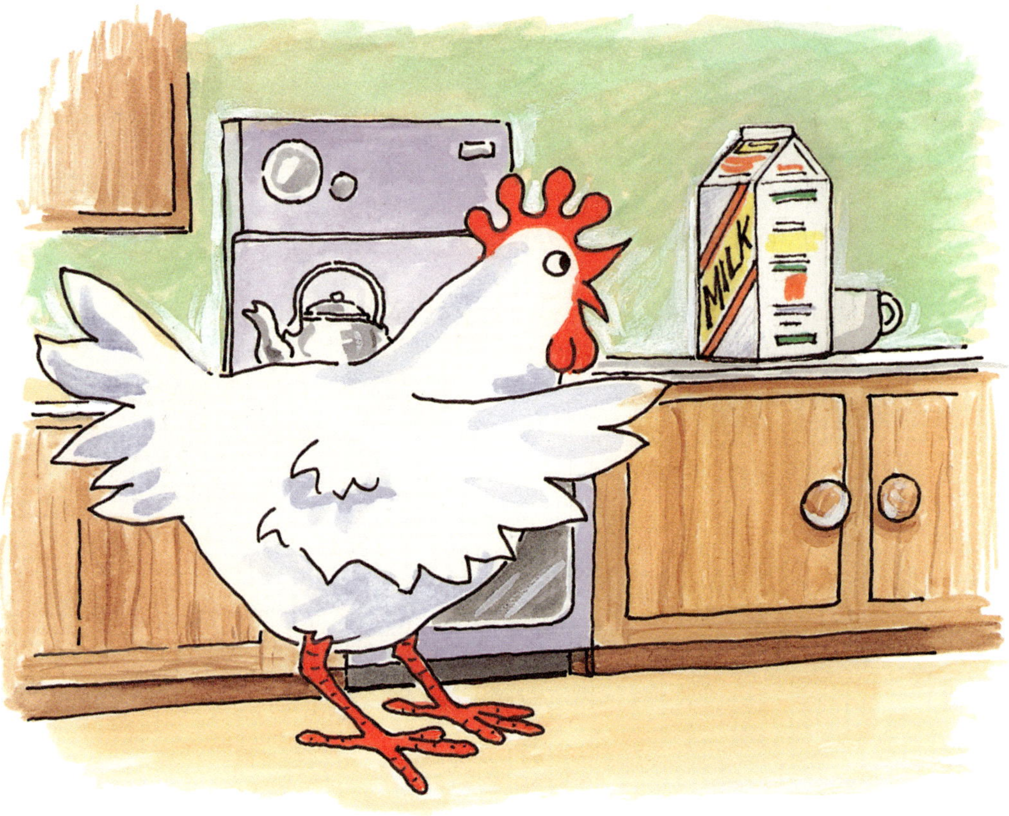

This is my milk.

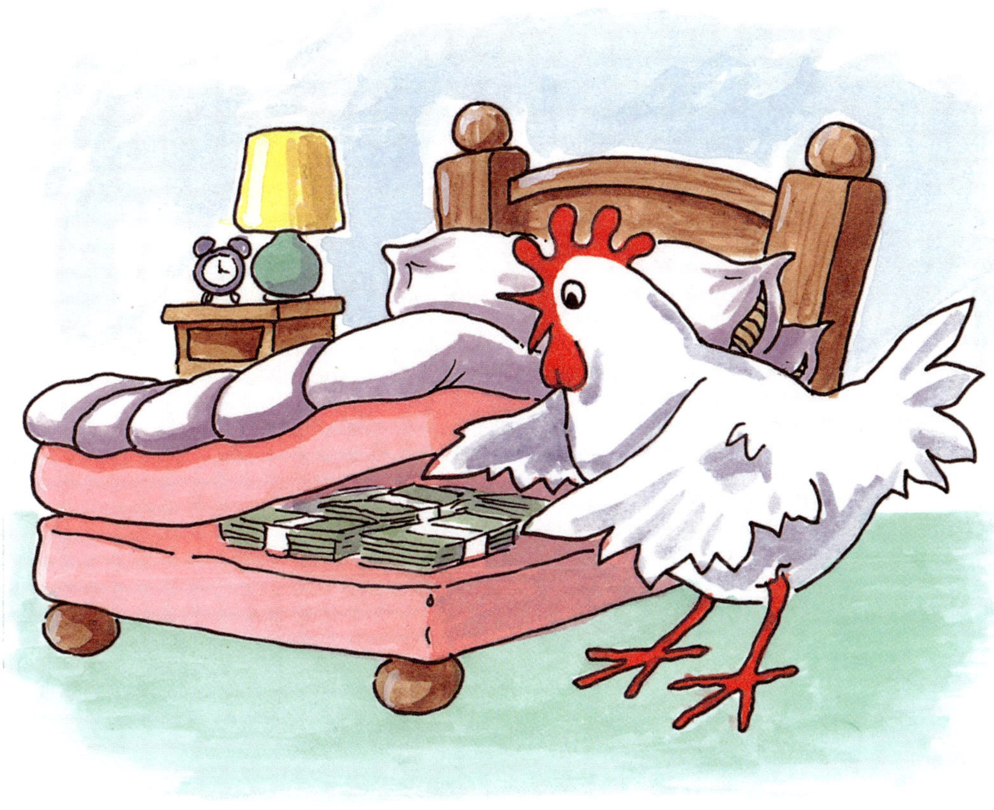

This is my money.

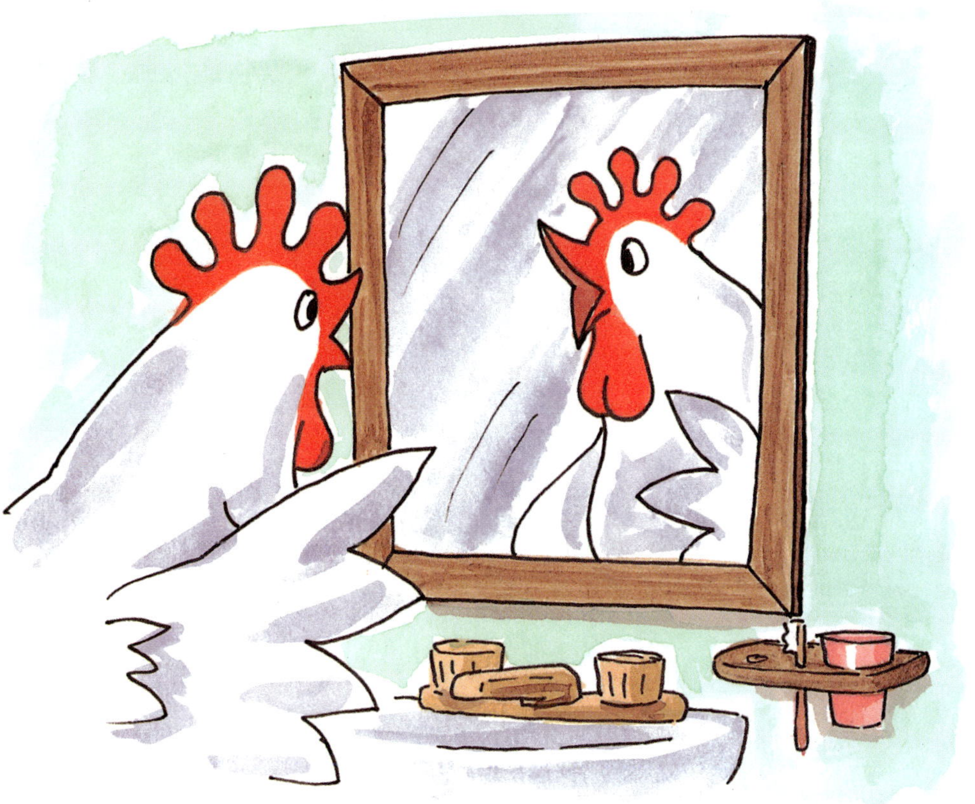

This is me!